ALTAR OF THE IMAGINATION

Marisa Urrutia Gedney

Finishing Line Press
Georgetown, Kentucky

Copyright © 2022 by Marisa Urrutia Gedney
ISBN 978-1-64662-879-7 First Edition
All rights reserved under International and Pan-American Copyright Conventions. No part of this book may be reproduced in any manner whatsoever without written permission from the publisher, except in the case of brief quotations embodied in critical articles and reviews.

Publisher: Leah Huete de Maines
Editor: Christen Kincaid
Cover Art: Diana Molleda
Author Photo: Gabrielle Messineo
Cover and Book Design: Diana Molleda

Order online: www.finishinglinepress.com
also available on amazon.com

Author inquiries and mail orders:
Finishing Line Press
PO Box 1626
Georgetown, Kentucky 40324
USA

TABLE OF CONTENTS

ALTAR OF THE IMAGINATION

First Quarter 9

Her First Tortilla 10

Altar of the Imagination 12

What Happens When A Bird Eats Lead? 16

Her Name Doesn't Say Enough 18

Casa Princesa 20

SPIRIT TECHNOLOGIES

Who is on Fire? 24

Wind is Wind 27

The Concha Called and Asked, "What's Up With You?" 29

SNAKES AND LADDERS

Salvatierra, I Know You 32

Fire to Glass to Water 34

El Jardinero Azul 35

Sing In Other Worlds 39

The Orange of the City 40

At What Point Do I Overflow You? 41

To my nana, Yolanda Leon Gedney,
thank you for teaching me how to live.

ALTAR OF THE IMAGINATION

FIRST QUARTER

I woke up with the moon on my forearm

a sealed portal to a slow passing.
You came, I know, Nana
like the night when you returned
like the way you told me as a child
that your parents lived on the moon.
What can it mean to retreat to somewhere so far away?
You are where you want to be
still, I turn to sorrow for safety

I plead O'Keeffe to paint
two ladders to the moon instead
so I can speak with you, Nana, beyond dreams
feel your touch on my face, scratch on my back

a bridge already exists, mijita
you don't even need to climb

everytime I look up to a first quarter
blue and white spirit
circling us
showing half
for me half for you
I know the party isn't over yet

third generation is where chaos stops
your survival cleared me for
action with ease
decisions with confidence
not the right to an education, but the privilege of pleasure

we land on the roof together
looking to the skies.

HER FIRST TORTILLA

Pastel lavender kernels of a fading sunset
not nuclear over the 710 apocalypse bright
this corn is claiming colors
of what the hills get painted when the sun goes down,
nothing to be scared of in the subtlety of
glowing to say goodnight

corn for tortillas
simple cheap food for the kids
to spread butter and sprinkle salt on
but she was stubborn even when
there was no point to be made anymore
when alcohol was no longer the problem
It was for her
the fear of it coming back

she packed her metate away, gave up her muscles
turned to sourdough bread instead
San Francisco in a plastic bag
never looked back
to the lunch making days
if she couldn't work she put her
worth into lunches and dinners
nourishing to fix him
after so many nights of

fresh
warm
pressed
hands
pride
hate

she found out he sold them at work
for money to buy booze
she could have hit him with the comal
wished one of them dead
at least

so never, ever again
turned tortilla
into tort-ee-yuh
not in her tongue
the one nuns and her mother thought was stupid, so they beat her
she dropped out
like a disease
the ones she grew from stress seeping into her joints
no pancakes either, nothing
round or soft
she wished for a machine to make waffles
or bread dipped in egg and cinnamon,
new requests so people would stop
asking her for that old one

those colors of corn grown so close to the ocean
that purple, that pink
the colors she asked us to wear to her funeral
so beautiful maybe
it would have been time
to make her first tortilla.

ALTAR OF THE IMAGINATION

"Can someone inherit a craving?"
—Sandra Cisneros

I
This is an altar of the imagination
I do not pray here
I will not be inheriting your
loss and fears or love for watermelon and mice
I want to remember when I couldn't breathe
and not picture you unknowingly
passing that choke onto me

this is an altar of the imagination
stop to smell the fire rocks that burn away
the trash overflowing in your basket.
I am mine here
I do not kneel in prayer or wait
I yell
in soft tones

steal me a peach
run through front yards to
slash juicy flesh
start to break your rules
even the ones that tell you how to be good

really you are bad, so let it be
your honesty balances out harm

your malcriada is innocent anyway
it's true in you, so let it die a prisoner leaving notes
for what once was
but never lived
not in this life,
not on this altar.

II

Marzipan is chalky, disgusting even
but I enjoy its soft colors
how almonds can be shaped by sugar
molded small and strange
sherbet is the only ice cream I can stomach
I collect rocks, write place names on them, dates I forget
one day they will go in a pyramid shaped vessel too
touch each one and hear the riverbed in Yosemite
the sea lions in Cambria
Santa Cruz slugs make no sounds, a sludgy yellow dance

yes, you can inherit a craving and always want more
I eat slow to pretend I don't want more than what fits on my plate
make cochinadas with leftovers
mix Catalina dressing and cottage cheese or
peanut butter and Sriracha on a corn tortilla
sugar goes well with everything

the body codes lifelong secrets
knowing exactly what will tear you down

and when
but what about fear, skipping a generation—how does that travel from your body to mine?
Faulty genes or increased risks
living behind a freeway wall
sending food to Farmer John's
receiving it back
frontyards in the radius of a battery waste plant
everyday repair had no chance
was anxiety meant to strike earlier when passed down to me?

Get it out of the way, she requested,
for her little peanut,
at twenty-five the mind has a better chance of bouncing
back than at forty-five.
And it did. Almost didn't leave the house just like her cells
that wanted to do their job of exact replica

I am not an imprint. I am not a signed number two

two metres of tight coils
two copies of each gene
there was never a chance
they picked up mistakes
good love can't repair faults
they thought it would look good on me,
a life looking out the window,
not closing the bathroom door, small spaces unsafe

it takes work to stop cell mutation
to change history
I could not protest, who would listen?

III
This is an altar of the imagination
one you can look up to
or at

share the sky with inherited burdens
clouds to hide behind
blue to stretch into, try on flashy
lightning
what is it like for so many to watch you at once?
No other choice but to hold the weather through the clash

I inherited a craving for control
I will not share the sky
I will not let you hold me
please be tender and know what I want
these aren't expectations, they are orders

I inherited a craving
to fix you
make you more
show you how far west you can go to
need me

I inherited a craving
to please.
Do my curls look better long or short?

How do you want your toast?
Will you be mad if I tell you what I really want?

I inherited a craving
to collect small things
destroy them too
clear this clutter
I want to keep nothing

what to do with this blood
passed down
I can learn better this time without rules
you taught me
to love

I want nothing.

WHAT HAPPENS WHEN A BIRD EATS LEAD?

You showed me a bird
if color is communication
I see nothing
how can I know in an instant it means love and hope?
I can't see the melanin of its intricate iridescence
or know why you sent a message via wings
is it busy grooming off radiation?

I saw two sets of Canadian Geese overhead
their honks chased away the mourning doves
who gets to lead and decide when to stop?
Late fog lifts as it heats up to 100 degrees, this morning the third day of fall
satisfying questions of who guides me: the bird

white doves hang on Whittier Blvd.
a one day line for Lolita's Tamales
what should I do with these birds?
Watercolor fluorescent wings, ok
dance with gallo feathers, sure
put them away in poster mail canisters to keep them safe from moths, yes
not take offense when the one danzante from San Jose
says my feathers are going in the wrong direction
a ceramic white swallow sits in front of me for years

what should I do with these birds?

I wish I could give you the hummingbirds too
with the crown mohawk of orange
spiking to bite the moon of paradise
winter blooms for such a tropical heat of a plant

in front of the Live Oak house protecting phobias
focused on the pain of a constricting throat and tight chest
I leaned on the spiral iron of the porch to breathe what you couldn't
lead from the leaking battery plant
pig carcass smoke from Farmer John's
what is it like to live inside dead animals

freezing bodies for food?
To thread bobbins, exhaust from inefficient machines
is that what makes a woman die at 73?
A man die less than a month after her?

The birds ate from the same poison
fifteen years later they test the dirt for the first time
you have to bring your soil to them
greed doesn't need proof
teenagers with several small dead siblings
children with leukemia know
mothers who live in hospitals
never talk about their dead children or leave Boyle Heights
this many cases of early cancer can not be normal
only death from guns make the headlines
this killer leads an easy massacre:
all four sisters get cancer

skeleton mija crown of feathers
they say, pheasant
but now each one merged with my thick human hair
I wear my glory high
next to a portrait of an artist
against her home
blackbird pinned to the wall

Birds that don't fly anymore
have other powers to see faraway near ones
call them through Apache
the jumps are high, squats that crack knees

a life breathes
if you've felt light as joyfully as the dark
you contain all of the earth
salt and air fly in you
and that's what sets you free

so do knowing mutators
what is the first to go in a bird's wing?
Does it start to lose its feathers from the inside?
Can it die as its flying over the water
gliding?

HER NAME DOESN'T SAY ENOUGH

Were you mad when your Indio daughter gave us a revolutionary name
a hard to say name
names with R's that roll—

and tanned her skin to
deep, dark brown, parted black hair
all the way down to her butt
there was no mistaking that she was a shiny happy Chicana fighting for her rights in
her own VW bus
introduced herself as Beverly and
white Black Brown, all were confused
it's not quite the movie star name you thought it was
where did a Beverly come from?
She drove from East LA to Commerce, knew she was poor
really poor
but had her NO accent tongue
perfect Spanish on the inside and her name,
no-ita can be added to that!
She's pure, three syllables of
you fit right in
you gave her this,
because she didn't come out with milky skin
or eyes like a messy blue storm
you gave her this,
and she passed it on
didn't you understand
what happens
when people get here?
They want to be
More
American
More
not what their skin
or voice
or smells
or sadness shows
were you mad when you found out
your granddaughter wishes to speak Spanish like it rolled right out, all natural, no

books, no photographic memory to learn the tenses

her name doesn't say enough
were you mad to find out
we are who we really are?

CASA PRINCESA

Clean up your river
little princess with no braids to pull you up by
how do you know you are Mestiza if
you look like no one
little one
who can't see the future
she has none
can't cook, fold clothes, or make a bed
came from nowhere
not meant for the time of the outside

we are fine
sky people
roasting
freezing
working at 5am your time
in the clouds
even in particles of water you can't take a day off

I can not clean up two rivers
at once one, at the bottom of the Grand Canyon
two, falling into the Pacific Redwoods
even if we move between both as often as we need
the distance is just as long as the one from head to heart
and those veins work furiously

mix of sage
turned dead
in drought
"there is darkness and then there is darkness"
light enters both when there is an offering, but

I can't send cedar to San Francisco
or San Jose
all I have is a dying bush
purposeful burn
could go on for the whole day of rest
sending messages to everyone it was asked to

send something snake woman
sweep your bells
your skirt of tongues
or you're not really of both darkness and light
pure no
too much of one

use the part of the body that holds patience
and the revolutionary act of listening

not the ears

those are for adornment

not for devouring

a wild hand hits the drum
a new kind of palo makes music without knowing how to make music

you didn't teach me how to walk upside down,
how can I see that kind of light
arched doorways, white rainbows

water does the work of cleaning
both rivers are tart
white, murky

don't confuse this as dirty
if your milk comes from a tree
pick it, squeeze it, bathe in it

don't breathe it
this is not your air
run to find what you can suck in

where you go at night to hear nothing
not even church air is safe

god can not protect you

on either side of the canoe
too full and you'll tip

center is the safest

the Suez canal, controlled by two interests
contains no locks
side channels run
back to itself
a direct route
cut to pieces to create you.

WHO IS ON FIRE?

1.
Who is on fire?
In this house, everyone
contained under yawns or meows
in front of a T.V.

taught to spew, spark on
flames almost touching
each one stays singular
but learns the hues of all
I am blue then burnt
happens so fast
someone bring me water, put me out
stop this rage
this sun, this dance.

2.
He creates heat by clearing the ground down to bare earth
minimizes risk for uncontrollable fire
searches for dead wood
to avoid moisture, allows air
makes a nest
sparks birch bark and an alloy of metals

this is his survival
he goes in

I watch his attempts to pull himself out with a fire glove
thinking one half of the body charred can still work
but he crumbles so fast
float when you're tired
of throwing on more logs
prevent smoke
I know you've wanted a rest since the first time you sensed
helpless
you can't fix this, or anything
so climb

horizontal to gain strength
get a feel for hanging on
fingertips are useful
calves will push
you will get to the top
route chosen by highlighted rigor
softly spin down
you will never be able to do much damage
if you touch air with the intention to fall.

3.

I am the little one
you are the big one
grooves in collected kindling split so easily
a tear in the interiority of the last two generations
wet with shame
and guilt pop
bad logs

now I know you didn't want me to have this
a mix of all your sadness
I will create my own ashes
I don't need to live through yours
I am not even daydreaming
but I've been rolling around in these piles of abundant fear
thinking this was part of my inheritance
release this error of holding onto the wrong treasure
I did not want to be selfish and turn away from the unsightly
I was taught to appreciate gold and the fake stuff too
you make beauty with what you can afford
pawn shops, QVC, pow-wows

I am the little one
you are the big one
when I give this back to you
please burn it away
small candles can last for at least six hours
two generations behind me
if I can give mine back through flame, you can too

I do this work for you

I want to leave
not hide
the difference is so clear to me
like the transparency of heat rising
as I burn up don't let anyone see what's under me
my middle is just as deadly.

WIND IS WIND

The breeze can not stand itself
viejitas bundled, slow mornings down 1st St.
A $2.50 cup of champurrado
worth the bite

wind is wind
it can not be anything else

to be filled with air in natural motion
is to know what direction your wild takes you
to know what air is between you and who you do not want to be
the temperature and speed is your precise refusal
reluctance, a hood to cover that small patch on the back of your head you still worry
about smashing in
when really, you could use a hard hat

really,
nothing can protect you from
all the ways you
do not want to be

wind is wind
it can not be anything else
the wind does not come from the sky
it is the sky
form

its nature is to be destructive
it changes course in patterns, to rise

the wind has never left the sky

tall firs are made to sway
monster garbage trucks are made to collect and scare away with noise both were
built with a mask
so were you
you can wear it with your eyes still showing

ehecatl
called in for more than a day
cleaned the air to make way

when stillness turns to shaking
just be
slow and long
between wind and water
coming from Mexico and reuniting with abalone
land and sea
dirt is called sand
wet dirt is called mud
smoke is always smoke
your prayer will land where it was sent
the wind will do its work.

THE CONCHA CALLED AND ASKED, "WHAT'S UP WITH YOU?"

We are here
where are you?

First call
The cuentista tale
Who's the great grandmother of this joke or sad story?

Second call
mystery woman tells herself to stay on the right path
where is it easier to get lost, the desert or the mountain?

Third call
man asks for spring
should he still grow a garden of food and medicine in a drought?

Fourth call
lift up this baby to the light
what's her name and did she come from the moon?

Noise gets pulled and turned on edge
when the concha blows

sirens are only for those waiting
this alarm is silent
even when the call is loud
dizzy from blowing air to be heard,
it never comes back

even if your canto is ugly
and it is
divine confusion
wherever you have to make the call
this wind instrument is not for you

get back to work
adjust to the blue
bottom

you can breathe here too
when you call back, say,
"I'm a wild woman
keeping the night
keeping the day
I wake up early to do a lot for you."

Give it what you got like a bat outta hell
the hell it's been to, or all of them.

SNAKES AND LADDERS

SALVATIERRA, I KNOW YOU

Snake catches us with eye and tongue
as we hike past the avocado grove
toward goats and bougainvillea
I would have kept walking too close to say
hi honey

not knowing clarity warns danger
I should have known the quick spin and
aggressive protection of a smooth body
I am fire serpent when I dance, too
with a flower growing out of my back, you too Xochitl?
I am not you, she says,
pero, hi honey

you say, stay there while I get a stick
I mistake your staff for a sword
ask you not to get involved with her skin,
do not touch what you do not know

both of them roll their eyes at me

I see him as snake
his search for a long enough piece of wood, she approves:
Salvatierra, I know you
hi honey
thank you for respecting my speed
not expecting me to move
or grow for you,
we do not molt on command
play with me next to underwater cholla

I don't hear any of this conversation,
my mind is on getting to the other side
only able to read obvious signage:
I question the barbed wire
why is the fine so high for picking fruit?

She allows us to walk past

eyes following eyes until
we're the same distance away from the horizon
we don't get sent back to zero
his skill is success this close to mountain and sky

Salvatierra, I know you

what redeemed me this time?
Not luck, but
his trust in the time it takes

one more chance to play
save the earth,
in soundless stillness
save me.

FIRE TO GLASS TO WATER

I'm mad you haven't built me glass out of those flames

why no vase or perfume bottle?
No sculpture for the hummingbirds
to sip from and poop on,
a window to catch the sun and make the air dance

produce prisms for me

I want you to make me light
you are a maker
make me

those all the time
hot hands of yours
do a lot of good

take the hint
of my hands
small and cold
like sand at Moonstone Beach
only illuminated after a wash
a long bath so the liver gets warm again

warm, let's swim there

you need a bucket of water

lift
you aren't giving yourself
sip

what it takes to burn

slow breaking tides take me heavy
I can barely keep my head above
thrilled, laughing from the pull in all directions
fully clothed, you jump in to save me

a dangerous wash onto the dry rocks.

EL JARDINERO AZUL

On the car ride past the San Gabriel mountains
we leave what we think is beautiful, enter
what we always dismissed
so many places to climb
your new waterproof map of peaks
reveals the backdrop of your childhood
not as desolate and devoid as you thought
we pass strip malls, a roadside metal mammoth, a neon burger sign where the north
slopes into Fontana
where the dread rolls in

you are not even in this car
your thoughts are on fixing your family
the weight you didn't know was strapped to you when you left
beyond the pale
what it takes to hold up the fence from faraway cities
your arms must be long, your muscles trained
to strain

you dutifully dug deep
rebuilt the wooden fence every summer with your dad
when hundred degree heat blew
annual destruction you counted on

this is how you learned to turn into a bronze god
working hard will not produce sustained success
to let your skin turn its darkest shade will not bring you any closer
will not bring any relief to what you endured
what you endure
a California seal framed on your parent's wall
a colored pencil drawing of a foul lagoon
looks so small next to quinceñera photos you are not in
will do nothing to push out
traumas of migration

you planted lemon trees, patiently waited for the nopal
agreed upon permissive neglect, the no-rules of your ma and pa
a father can not be heard from behind the wheel of a big rig
asleep off the side of the highway

in the middle of the state
a mother can not understand you when she is moving borders for sisters, fathers,
brothers

you never saw limits
you made your own
crossed the only imaginary line you knew
every summer, hours in a long line of cars to come back home
where piñatas hang on backs
no lessons in waiting
left to forsake

you nail wood
grained with abandonment
to protect yourself from what really hurts
your skin can handle sun and wind
but can not touch what it means to be the one no one understands your vocabulary
and quick wit in English don't mean anything here
they don't understand how late you stay up to write lessons
too tired of saving someone who keeps going back in
behind the tallest fence he could put himself behind
razor wire coiling at the top, just to be sure
safer inside he says, as his every move is watched

your refusal to allow failure
they read as arrogance
when you start your own garden to grow
what you need to vine up past the betrayal
you let the cilantro blossom to collect its seeds
use the inherited molcajete for something

replanted from the rancho your dad left behind
you think he plants for food and medicine
these memories you eat grow you a crown of thorns you were gifted
when you moved as far
from the desert as you could

in this car ride to where you avoid going often,
you are silent to me while you plan to mow the lawn
pick up your mail, repair every computer in the house,

wonder if you will have to stop someone from getting in the car after a day of drinking

my thoughts are on you
your quiet I read as relaxation
you are mine again for this brief ride
let's sing
I hum to Violetta Parra
you translate her heartbreak for me
this song set in a garden I think is about growing love
para mi tristeza violeta azul
a desire for desperate relief
wishing her flowers to nurse her back

remedio para mi pena
aquí plantaré el rosal
de las espinas más gruesas
tendré lista la corona
para cuando en mi te mueras

I hear La Jardinera as
cultivation
voy a cultivar la tierra
assume that descriptions of
planting pink roses and violet petals falling
means love,
I mistake burial for growth

I confuse words I think I know after eight years of Spanish,
three generations of forced forgetting:

Cometona for the name of your chameleon, Comelona who craves crickets
they call you my pareja,
I see you as a bird and don't question why a couple is compared to flight
sing, parajo, sing

you understand the subtle ways my scrambled
photographic mind embarrasses me

I can not know the meaning from the content,
pesadilla

I see a fish wrapped in corn
when I read the definition as nightmare
I don't trust my sense to guess, I can not read context
I can laugh quickly when you point out my mistakes
but I can't translate when you remove yourself

I try to look up the words to fill in your blanks
jamming something in that does not fit
I do not know what questions to ask
to help you define yourself

what pain do you need to bury?
What do you want to forget with each tilling of the soil?
Peel what you grow for me
I need you to tell me the words you
use for suffering
can not be translated

our garden shares an orange hue
that doesn't require a fence
so we can watch the tumbleweeds gain speed as they travel.

SING IN OTHER WORLDS

I miss you on the way to work
Jefferson Airplane says *I'm so full of love I could burst apart and start to cry*
every morning
deep cries, I have to catch my
breathe
swallow
I can feel your skin next to mine at 4am
already waking up in blank dreams with a migraine, nauseous

I watch you with eyes closed, even then no peace
the only hours you are still, here
your bones are
used up
nothing left

when I asked you to find yourself
I didn't know that would mean you would need to leave

you never asked me if you could move
away
you never asked me to give up love,
a ghost to yourself

please please listen to me

I didn't agree to this strange loneliness
to be with you but without you, always

a plea, a countdown to when you have time to return

If you can sing in other worlds
I want to hear you.

THE ORANGE OF THE CITY

When I smell the orange of the city
I think of you inhaling me
so close and I can't see you

AT WHAT POINT DO I OVERFLOW YOU?

"You have to make up your mind about what you're going to love."
—Nikki Giovanni

You throw away the most important
letter you'll ever write
not even a reason for the disposal
toss so easily the love you have for a child
a photo satisfies you
I worry about what you will
want to get rid of when I am too much

at what point do I overflow you?

I will hold on to any word
to see you as form in letters
is how I touch your soul
but you haven't picked up a pen in years
how will you remind me we need rice?
How can I know you think of me at 5am-when you are the only one so awake in the dark?
The clues I am looking for
in how warm you can get me
I want to know if you use water or sky
to measure
the depth of your feelings
which ocean is the deepest?
How would you arrange the stars for me?
I will collect your words to give back to you
so you can see how the accumulation
of how sweetness stacks
how to bind a book
I will sew, print, press into you
until I am too big for you to toss.

Acknowledgements

Thank you to the editors who published this poem in a different form: Her Name Doesn't Say Enough: Statement Magazine.

Tremendous gratitude to the writing teachers that shaped these works and helped me be a more honest writer: Chris Abani, Juan Felipe Herrera, Denise Chávez, Eduardo C. Corral, and Lorna Dee Cervantes.

Thank you, Hedgebrook, where I was fed, housed, and had beautiful time alone to write what I needed to write.

I acknowledge Jorge Segura and his trust in me to share this part of our lives. I thank him for his dedication to our relationship, uncoupling, and love evolution and am deeply grateful we are family, still.

To Xochitl-Julisa Bermejo for running Women Who Submit and all the inspiration and information she gave me to apply for residencies and submit to publications.

Vickie Vértiz for encouraging me and bringing me with her. Her guidance and generosity opened opportunities and this book wouldn't exist without her.

To Grupo Xiuhcoatl, my jefes and fire snakes I dance and pray in circle with, thank you for showing me these ways to pray, for your gifts of medicine and tools, for handing me my first concha and for being my spiritual family.

Diana Molleda, thank you for turning these poems into a book and spending time shaping my words into a beautiful object.

Kenji C. Liu, Emilie Coulson Salgado, Vickie Vértiz, it is my greatest honor to have you as part of this creation, thank you for seeing me through my art.

To my mom and dad, Albert Leon Gedney and Beverly Urrutia Gedney, for teaching and giving me everything I needed and more, for showing me how to tell stories and nurture what we love.

To my sister Ramona for all the ways she attempted to thrive with courage. Her life was her testimony.

About the Author

Marisa Urrutia Gedney (she/her) named one of Forbes Magazine's top 30 under 30 in Education, 2012, spent a 14 year career using writing in the classroom as a social justice practice for identity work and strived to make college access more equitable. She directed and published a series of Ethnic Studies books that tell overlooked histories written by students in Boyle Heights.

As a Sahumadora in Danza Azteca, she practices fire as her spirit technology and transmutes grief and transgenerational trauma in her poetry. Poetry publications include *Women, Mujeres, Ixoq: Revolutionary Visions* and *Coiled Serpent: Poets Arising from the Cultural Quakes & Shifts in Los Angeles*. She was invited by former U.S. Poet Laureate Juan Felipe Herrera to read at the Los Angeles Library series, ALOUD, and has received a Writers in Residence at Hedgebrook, studied at the Postgraduate Writers' Conference at Vermont College of Fine Arts, Voices of Our Nation, and Las Dos Brujas.

Experiencing significant loss from an early age, she dedicates her life to normalizing the grief experience and is a volunteer with the COVID Grief Network providing 1-1 and small group grief support.

As Co-Founder of, Your Truth At Work, a BIPOC healing space for women & gender expansive advocates who demand and desire equity and justice at work, she supports people to continue disrupting white supremacy culture in the workplace and healing from its harm.

www.ingramcontent.com/pod-product-compliance
Lightning Source LLC
LaVergne TN
LVHW041559070426
835507LV00011B/1193